# A MUST READ TRADITIONAL AND CULTURAL WEDDING CEREMONY MADE EASY AND INTERESTING

## SAVE THIS DYNASTY FROM FURTHER DAMAGES

Dr. Lansana Nyalley

BALBOA.
PRESS

A DIVISION OF HAY HOUSE

Balboa Press books may be ordered through booksellers or by contacting:

Balboa Press
A Division of Hay House
1663 Liberty Drive
Bloomington, IN 47403
www.balboapress.com
1 (877) 407-4847

Because of the dynamic nature of the Internet, any web addresses or links contained in this book may have changed since publication and may no longer be valid. The views expressed in this work are solely those of the author and do not necessarily reflect the views of the publisher, and the publisher hereby disclaims any responsibility for them.

The author of this book does not dispense medical advice or prescribe the use of any technique as a form of treatment for physical, emotional, or medical problems without the advice of a physician, either directly or indirectly. The intent of the author is only to offer information of a general nature to help you in your quest for emotional and spiritual well-being. In the event you use any of the information in this book for yourself, which is your constitutional right, the author and the publisher assume no responsibility for your actions.

Any people depicted in stock imagery provided by Getty Images are models, and such images are being used for illustrative purposes only. Certain stock imagery © Getty Images.

Print information available on the last page.

ISBN: 978-1-9822-3030-2 (sc)
ISBN: 978-1-9822-3031-9 (e)

Balboa Press rev. date: 06/25/2019

# Contents

MY UNDERSTANDING OF THE TRADITIONAL AND CULTURAL MARRIAGE AS GENERALLY PRACTICED BY MANY OF THE REGIONS AND TRIBES IN SIERRA LEONE, WEST AFRICA, ESPECIALLY THOSE OF THE MENDE TRIBE.

# A Brief Background of the Author

## BIRTHPLACE

My name is Lansana Nyalley (Ph.D.). I was born in Bombohun in November 1952 and grew up in Daru, Jawi Chiefdom, Kailahun District, Eastern Province, Sierra Leone, West Africa.

## EDUCATION

## PRIMARY SCHOOL

I learnt Arabic at home with my father for the early ten years of my life. I started Western Education much later at the then District Council Primary School, Daru (DC School Daru) from the third term in 1963 and finished in 1966. The School is now called Kailahun District Council School (KDCS), Daru. I completed classes one to five and took the Common Entrance Examination in class five. From my Arabic background, I was able to quickly memorize daily teaching lessons and materials. Thus, I was able to gain double promotions which quickened my primary school years from seven to only three years. I sat to and passed what was then called Common Entrance Examinations (for high school entrance), which is now called National Primary School Examination (NPSE) and passed to enter form one in the Kenema Government Secondary (KSS), Kenema, in 1966.

## SECONDARY SCHOOLS

I attended KSS from 1966 to 1968, forms one to three.

I transferred to Christ The King College (**C.K.C.**), in Bo, in 1968. The transfer was primarily to do basic science subjects offered in secondary schools at the time such as: chemistry, physics and biology, as individual subjects as compared to taking them together at **KSS** at the **Ordinary Level-O' Level**, now called **West African Senior Secondary Certificate Examination, WASSCE,** for college entrance as one subject under the heading **General Science**. After attending forms four through five, I took the **O' Level** in 1972.

I was unable to get the complete passes for the college entering requirements that year. I repeated form five at the Kissy Brook Ahmadiyya Secondary School, Kissy, Freetown, Sierra Leone in 1973 and completed the college entering requirements.

I attended Fourah Bay College in 1974 in the Engineering Department. I failed to continue my education there.

## COLLEGE DEGREES

I arrived in the United States of America (USA) on the 29th January 1976.

I started the Bachelor of Science degree in Chemistry (B.Sc.) at the then Bowie State College (now Bowie University) in 1977 and completed it in 1980 at the Howard University, Washington DC.

The Masters and Doctorate degrees in Organic or Medicinal Chemistry were completed from 1980 to 1983 and then from 1991 to 1996 respectively, all at Howard University, Washington District of Columbia (Washington DC) USA.

## WORK EXPERIENCE

**ASSITANT PROFESSOR OF ORGANIC CHEMISTRY**: I taught at Rowan University (Rowan College at the time), New Jersey, USA, as Assistant Professor of Organic Chemistry from 1996 to 1998.

**ADJUNCT PROFESSOR OF ORGANIC CHEMISTRY, 1998 TO 2011**. I transferred and taught Organic Chemistry at George Mason University as Adjunct Professor of Chemistry from 1998 to 2011. I taught summer schools at some other universities and colleges.

**PART-TIME HIGH SCHOOL TEACHER 1999 TO 2011**. I taught basic mathematics as part time teacher in a middle school in the DC Public School System from 1999 to 2011.

**PATENT AND TRADEMARK EXAMINER, PATENT AND TRADEMARK OFFICE (PTO), VIRGINIA, WASHINGTON DC 2011 TO 2012.**

I examined Patent applications and recommended acceptance or denial to my Supervisor for his subsequent final action.

**DEPUTY EDUCATION MINISTER AT THE MINISTRY OF EDUCATION, SCIENCE AND TECHNOLOGY FROM 2007 TO 2012.** Served as a Deputy Education Minister with specific responsibilities and duties at the Ministry of Education, Science and Technology, New England, Freetown, Sierra Leone.

# Dedication

I say thank you to God Almighty for given me the idea, opportunity, strength, courage, good health and guidance as I write. I also thank Him profusely for protecting all the members of my family, relatives and friends and for all of us been at where we are today by His Will. I pray for God's mercy for all those who have passed away. May God continue to be with us all now and always. Amen.

Further, I dedicate this Booklet to my late:

- Father- Pa Musa Nyalley.
- Mothers- Haja Watta Sannoh Sheriff; Haja Monjama Sannoh Nyalley; Baindu Seyba

Sannoh and Fodey Hawa Sojey Kanneh Nyalley for all the troubles I put them through just to be who I am today,

Additionally, I dedicate this work to my nuclear family which includes:

- Madam Monjama Nyalley and the children: Haja Monjama Bona Nyalley; Lansana Senesie Nyalley; Haja Watta Bona Nyalley; Baindu Wuya Bona Nyalley and
- Madam Elizabeth Nyalley and the children: Musa Nyalley, Saibattu Kallon and Mohamed Kallon.

To each one of you, individually and collectively, I say thank you for your unwavering love and support through those challenging years. Am sorry for my endless problems. Just know that I have always and will always love you in the name of God.

# Acknowledgement

There are so many other family members, friends, relatives, and supporters whose interactions with me created lasting impressions and impact in my life. Naming all of them will be impossible for me to do. Yet I will not be happy if I do not name at least some of them. I apologies to the many others that will not be mentioned by name here.

My current immediate family support base:

- Mr. and Mrs. Momoh Takaa and Fatmata Vandy.
- Mr. and Mrs. Mohamed Nyalley and Mariama Sheriff.

- Mr. and Mrs. Senesie Sheriff and Fulaha Nyalley
- Mr. and Mrs. Mohamed and Haja Monjama Kamara.
- Mr. and Mrs. Mohamed Tagameh and Baindu Seyba Nyalley.
- Mr. Patrick Keifa Vandy (PK).
- Mrs. Elizabeth Nyalley.
- Mrs. Monjama Nyalley.
- Mr. and Mrs. Moinina and Haja Agnes Sawi.
- Mr. and Mrs. Abdul Keita and Taway Tejan.
- Mr. and Mrs. Sulaiman and Faridas Sannoh.

Other family members, colleagues and peer groups including:

- Mr. and Mrs. Sulaiman and Faridas Sannoh
- Madam Matilda Simbo
- Madam Amie Aruna
- Madam Marion Cole
- Mr. and Mrs. Mohamed and Cordilia Sannoh

- Mr. and Mrs. Mohamed Sannoh and Mary Momoh
- Mr. Edmond Bockarie Sannoh
- Mr. Abu Sannoh
- Mr. and Mrs. Ansu and Fatmata Soni
- Mr. and Mrs. Yopoi and Patricia Alpha
- Dr. and Mrs. Sheku and Fatmata Idriss
- Alhaji and Mrs. Sheku and Fatmata Tarawally
- Mr. and Mrs. Kai and Mariama Sawi Baba James
- Mr. and Mrs. Umaru Vermunya and Fatmata Sheriff
- Dr. and Mrs. James and Sowue Senesie
- Mr. and Mrs. Ernest and Doris Pekanyande
- Mr. Ali Foh
- Honorable Victor Foh, former Vice President
- Mohamed and Mery Tarawally
- Mr. and Mrs. Philip and Mamie Pekanyande
- Mr. and Mrs. Lansana Steady Bongo and Jarai Sheriff
- Mrs. and Mrs. Evelyn and Dauda Bangura
- Mrs. Mariama and John Brewa
- Madam Juliet Anthony

- Mr. and Mrs. Al-Hassan and Xemana Koroma
- Mr. Victor Tarmoh
- Mr. Mohamed Sulaiman
- Mr. Alie Bundu
- Mr. and Mrs. John and Betty Sandy
- Mr. and Mrs. Cilaty and Regina Dabor
- Mr. and Mrs. Victor and Adama Wuya
- Mr. and Mrs. Lansana and Fatmata Sawi
- Madam Nematu Silla
- Madam Jestina Kuyembeh
- Madam Christiana Namisa Koroma
- Mr. and Mrs. Mattin and Fatmata Lahai
- Madam Mamie Jenneh Fofana.
- Madam Mamie Massah Sheriff; Sao Baindu Sannoh
- Yatta Seyba Sannoh; Hawa Sannoh; Fatty? Miatta Kebba
- Mr. and Mrs. Alfred and Amie Sannoh Ansumana
- Haja Jattu Seyba Sannoh.
- Mr. and Mrs. Festus and Jattu Musa
- Mr. and Mrs. Sheikh Alie and Haja Hawa Rogers.
- Madam Mamie Kavie Sheriff.

- President Rosaline Bangura and the entireTegloma Organization members, especially the Washington DC Tegloma Chapter family members.
- Mrs. Fatmata Mansaray
- Dr. and Mrs. Alghasim and Amie Jah
- Mr. Joseph N'Gaojia
- Mr. Joseph Fefegula
- Mr. Sheku Foday.
- Mr. Mustapha Conneh
- Mr. Ahmed Carter
- Mr. Sumory Alpha.
- Mr. Kangoma Sheriff.
- Mr. and Mrs. Brima and Gbessay Kambay.
- Messrs. Alvin S. Koroma; Bobson V. Dassama; Lansana Kebenia Sannoh; Sylvester Koroma; Mohamed B. Kamara; Lansana K. Dukulay, Ansumana Fofana; Akido Konneh, Chief Samai Bao; Chief Patrick Tangar; P.C. Chief Musa Ngombukla Kallon; friends of Dr. Lansana Nyalley, the people and towns of Jawi, Daru; Bombohun; Benduma; Njala, Willo, Malema, Madu, Dea, Jaluahun, Upper Bambara and many other people and places.

# Chapter 1
# Prephase

In this Booklet, my primary intendment is to provoke greater minds to begin the debate on **standardizing the Traditional and Cultural Marriage**, especially as practiced within the Mende Culture. In Sierra Leone, the practice is mostly identical among the regions and tribes, except with some minor variations neither here nor there. Establishing a standard format for performing the ceremony will help to sustain the chore values and probably increase the interest and fun pertaining thereto.

I must hurry to emphasize, if not already obvious, that I have no background in the requisite discipline or training to write this booklet. However, my intense and tenacious love for the tradition and culture is the driving force that motivates this writing.

It is my argument that this deep rooted and admirable dynasty is dying from endless challenges emanating from changes and practices at the mercy of some people who either do not actually know how to perform the ceremony correctly or are in desperate hurry to finish it quickly or both. Why do they do it at all?

## IF IT IS WORTH DOING, THEN IT IS WORTH DOING IT RIGHT

It stands to reasoning that as time changes, certain unavoidable and necessary changes are generally forced upon us either by society or nature or both. That is a given. However, notwithstanding, some of those changes, if not controlled now, are likely to threaten to deform the basic and chore values of the processes, procedures and beauty of our Traditional and Cultural Marriage, which could, more likely, render it meaningless. We are, therefore, required to make every serious effort to resist those destructive changes and to work as a team to preserve, protect and defend those values inherent therein and prevent it from being rendered meaningless. God forbids.

While I admit that it might not be enough for this one Booklet to completely eradicate the years of abuse, it will be a beauty if it can contribute to the beginning of formalizing, standardizing and simplifying the marriage processes, Practices and procedures pertaining to the Tradition and Culture. I am open to additional suggestions and corrections to enhance the intendment. Please read further.

# Chapter 2

# Introduction

Traditional and Cultural Marriage is as old as I know it. It has the blends of mostly cultural practices and those of Islamic and a tiny bit of Christian values and influences.

Strongly willed by tradition and some Islamic guides, Traditional and Cultural Marriage was a final marriage concluded at the end of the ceremony. I do not know about you, but that was how my father married my mother years ago. Ceremonial weddings at the Mosque or Church may be compelled upon Participants either by legal options or individual choices. Today, Traditional and Cultural Marriage is, at least to some people, considered an engagement. Wow! I have been told by some Islamic scholars that, especially when the process involves some Quranic recitations, is the main form of marriage the Quran demands on Muslims in this part of the World.

Despite the volume of this Booklet or explanations, only few major steps, as listed below, are required to guide, protect and preserve the process:

- **To initiate the process**, at least one informal meeting between some of the family members or parents of the bride and groom, initiated by a groom's family member (**stranger, visitor, or guest**) is required. At least a member of the groom's family creates contact with at least one member of the bride's family. This contact transmits the interest of the groom's family to the family of the bride leading to the first meeting named above. This meeting is intended to express the interest of the groom's family in the daughter; meet with some of the bride's family members; learn some of their requirements; get a primary host from the bride's family to guide the groom's family during the period leading to the formal meeting and to set the date, time and place for the formal marriage ceremony.

- Identify the biological parents; god parents; spokesperson(s); family-head; to prepare the Calabash; prepare the envelopes for greetings; prepare gowns for the biological parents and god parents; provide the engagement ring and prepare the dowry (the money to marry the woman with). Etc. **Generally speaking, the dowry is any amount the bride and groom agree to**.

- **THE BRIDES FAMILY MUST ALSO HAVE READY THE FOLLOWING ITEMS (HOSTS)**: God parents; biological parents; items to welcome the guests/visitors; envelopes for the biological parents and god parents; family head; spokesperson; envelopes, water, kolanuts and some envelopes to receive the groom's biological parents and god parents Etc.

- **IN CERTAIN CASES,** the Groom's family is required to either pay a fix sum of money for the wedding day or finance the entertainment, including feeding, on the wedding day.

- **ARRIVE AT THE MEETING PLACE EARLY AND BE PREPARED TO SPEND SOME TIME, MONEY AND ANSWER QUESTIONS AT THE DOOR** (where necessary), TO IN ORDER TO BE ALLOWED TO ENTER.

- **ONCE INSIDE**, THE HOSTS CALL FOR THE OPENING PRAYERS.

- **HOW THE MEETING BEGINS?** The eldest or spokesperson of the Hosts ask: who called us? **ONLY A MEMBER OF THE BRIDE'S FAMILY WILL ANSWER.** The Visitor's Primary Host answers: I did, but I was directed by these people, pointing to the Visitors.

- **FIRST GREETINGS WITH ONE ENVELOPE TO REPORT AS VISITORS**. At this time, **there is no**

**mention of brothers, sisters etc. because there has not been any mention of a woman or flower**. THE VISITOR'S SPOKESPERSON WILL THEN SAY, BEFORE WE GO ANY FURTHER, MAY WE GET A PRIMARY HOST TO GUIDE US? When given, a brief familiarization meeting is held with the Primary Host. **FROM THIS POINT ON, BOTH FAMILIES CAN OFFICIALLY TALK TO EACH OTHER ONLY THROUGH THEIR SPOKESPEOPLE.** The Primary Host presents the first envelope (money), kolanut, a bottle of water and possibly a bottle of liquor (for non-Muslims) to present the Visitors as Guests of the family. The Hosts and Hostesses will give identical things to the Visitors, welcome them as well as give them seats.

* **INTRODUCTIONS AND THE SECOND SETS OF ENVELOPES**. The eldest or spokesperson of the Hosting family again ask through the Primary Host: who are you and where do you come from? After getting the permission

to speak, the Spokesperson of the Visitors, through the Primary Host, ask for permission to introduce the Visitors. That will be followed by the Hosts introducing themselves. At the end, the Visitor's Spokesperson obtain permission to present the second sets of envelopes. **Still, there is no mention of brothers and sisters for the same reason given above**.

- **THE THIRD SETS OF ENVELOPES, THE CALABASH AND THE RING**. The eldest or Spokesperson of the Hosts again ask: What are all these greetings for? The Primary Host answers, we have seen a woman or Flower in your house that we want. Hosts ask: who wants the woman? Do you want her for yourself? I want her for my son. May we see your son?

- **THE TIME HAS COME FOR THE GROOM TO ENTER THE HOUSE WITH DANCES AND TAKE A SEAT**. Questions and answers are exchanged.

- **SUBSEQUENTLY, IT WILL B TIME FOR THE BRIDE TO ENTER WITH MORE FANFARE**. After some women are rejected as not being of the right choice at the time, the actual bride is brought in. Questions and answers are equally exchanged.

- **STEPS TO MARRY**: befriend the woman, engage her with money and kolanut and the groom's family may end it here if all they came for was to engage (**put kola**) for the bride. The next few remaining steps is to completely marry her. It is important to note that the rest of the **bride's family members are given greeting envelopes only after the bride had accepted the love proposal and is been engaged for marriage**.

- **HOW THE CALABASH WALKS**? It is encouraged that the wedding Calabash is dressed and brought to the meeting place with jubilation by a virgin or a teenage girl. The god father of the groom gives the Calabash to the god mother of the bride.

She took it and show it to their entire family members as a marriage proposal to their daughter. She will then ask the bride: these people want to marry you. They gave us this calabash. Do you permit us to accept it? The bride answers, yes or turn to her family and say, I pass this Calabash on to you for your final guidance. The bride's god mother will then say, I will give you this Calabash. If you want them, you will accept it and then return it to us. If you do not want them, then do not accept it. The Calabash is then given to the bride. She accepts it and then return it to the god mother. Their family members will proceed to a secret location to open and check the contents of the Calabash. The will return with jubilation to show approval.

- **THE BLESSING OF THE RING BY EITHER THE IMAM OR PASTOR AS THE CASE MAY BE.**

- **I do not like** to use the word strangers to describe the groom's family members coming to visit because it tends to connote that the people are from Mass or have never been seen before strange. I will use **visitors** and **guests** instead. You may use strangers for the fun. I see no harm in using it.

It may be true that compelling social, economic and political demands, among many others, have forced some changes upon us. Some changes including but not limited to knocking on the door to enter; seeing a flower instead of a woman in the house; bringing more than one woman pretending them to be the bride and the bringing of a ring etc. Thank God, some central roots of the traditions have survived these onslaughts.

I have been told that years back, this was the process by which several other parents were married. The few changes above were not observed then. What can we do to preserve, promote and protect the Traditional and Cultural Wedding from further damages in the years ahead? It may be a difficult challenge, but someone must start it. That is where this Booklet comes in.

Like many of you, I have seen several aggressive religious scholars condemning some aspects of the process as against some teachings of their religions. In Islam, one of the duties required of the parents is to their children is to help them get a good spouse. That is why during the process, it is the god parents, on behalf of the biological parents, who ask for a wife or accept a marriage proposal to marry for the child. After the ring has been blessed and worn on the fingers, that will be the end of the Traditional and Cultural Wedding. Bringing several women pretending then to be the actual bride introduces an acceptable fun, joke and laughter to the process.

However, for some people, it may be the beginning of the western marriage.

## SOME ORIGINAL UNDERSTANDINGS AND PRACTICES HELPED TO HEIGHTENED RESPECT AND LOVE FOR THE CULTURE.

- A man or woman marries into the whole family, town or village and not just to the wife or husband.

- The wife is never directly given to the husband. The god father and mother ask to marry the woman for their son. Blood relatives, where possible, must represent god parents and biological parents. Parents help to find a wife or husband for the son or daughter as an influence from the Islamic teaching.

- It is not the practice in the culture for a woman to give another woman in marriage since, to start with, she already belongs to her husband's family.

- The god parents were always different from the biological parents. It was common for the maternal uncles to give the woman in marriage.

- There were only one sets of uncles and aunts. All the father's brothers were all fathers. All the father's sisters were all aunts (the only aunts). All the mother's brothers were uncles (the only uncles) and all the mother's sisters were mothers. The nuclear family structure of the west recognizes only the biological father, mother, brothers and sisters. All else are either uncles, aunts, grandparents, nephews or nieces etc.

- There was no knocking on the door for permission to enter because, for one thing, such marriages took place in townhalls, verandas or other open settings where there were hardly any doors.

- I do not know about yours, but my own village did not have flowers then. And

- Only the woman's (bride's) family would dictate the marriage processes and procedure. The general seating arrangements was for both families to sit down facing each other.

# Chapter 3
# Brief Explanations of some of the Key Positions

**FACE TO FACE MEETINGS**. The groom's family member befriends a member of the bride's family. He or she initiates contact with the bride's family. He or she becomes the unofficial Primary Host until officially selected to do so on the day of the wedding. At the request of the groom's family members, at least one face- to-face meeting between the members of the two families shall take place at a place selected by the bride's family before the wedding day. During this meeting, the Primary Host, experienced and knowledgeable in their cultural and traditional practices, is unofficially assigned to lead and guide the Visitors/Guests. The date, time and place are set. **Some families and villages have specific financial requirements that may be ironed out during this meeting. SOME ISLAMIC MARRIAGES ASK FOR NIKAO**- some special gift to be given to the woman by the husband later after the marriage such as a house, car, money or an animal-cow, goat, sheep etc.

**BIOLOGICAL PARENTS, GOD PARENTS, FAMILY HEADS AND SPOKESPERSONS** are selected on both sides.

**PREPARATION OF THE CALABASH**: Some groups add as many items to the Calabash as they want. Some basic things in there, as seen in some Islamic marriages include: the dowry, ring, at least one hundred tied kolanuts, another thirty to fifty tied kolanuts for the woman, Quran, prayer matt, a two yard "lappa" for the guard parent (who cared for the woman), needle, thread etc.

**GREETING ENVELOPES:** Three sets of greeting envelopes containing money must be prepared.

**The first set** has only one envelope, some kolanuts (10 to 15), a bottle of water and an alcoholic drink (if necessary). There are no mentions of a woman or her family members. This gift merely presents the Visitors as Guests to the family.

**The second** sets of envelopes are only for the members of the village, town, community members, elders and family members present at the meeting.

**The third sets of envelopes** after the woman has accepted the friendship request and has also been engaged. Then the third greetings begin with the biological parents; god parents; guard parent; grandparents and the rest.

**The fourth and final envelope** is to ask for the wife to move in and stay with the husband.

**Some towns and villages** have specific charges for marrying their daughter; moving her out of the village or staying in the village and for the chiefs.

**The family members of the bride**, in some cases, may ask for the groom and family to either wholly or partly finance the wedding event of pay a fix fee for it. It is normally the case for the bride's family to foot the feeding and entertainment bill.

# Chapter 4
# The Day of the Wedding (W-Day)

**SESSION ONE: OPENING PRAYERS**.

A member of the Hosting family to deliver or ask for the Visitors to give opening prayers.

**SESSION TWO**. **How does the meeting begin**? The **eldest of the Hosting family members or the spokesperson asks**: who called us? We are here.

**The Primary Host for the Visitors responds**: I did but I was told to do so by these people (pointing to the Visitors).

**Host's spokesperson**, looking at the Visitors then asks: did you call us? Here we are. Who are you?

**The spokesperson for the Visitors Responds**: Sirs and Madams, I greet you. Before I go any further, may I ask that you please give us a Primary Host to guide us? (This may have already been done before. However, it must be repeated to involve some family members who may not have been present in any of the previous meetings. It is a welcome repetition). The same previously appointed person or a new one will be given. A brief consultative meeting will be held to familiarize with the new Host. From this point on, the Visitors will address the Hosting family only through the Primary Host. The Hosting family will speak only through their spokesperson.

**First envelope to present the Visitors as Guests.** The visitor's spokesperson says to the Primary Host, through you, we present ourselves as Guests to this family, **BUT TO WHOM CAN WE**

**NOW PRESENT OURSELVES?** The Hosting family then points to someone among them as to whom the Visitors are to report. Then the Visitors through the Primary Host, pass on the envelope, kolanut, bottle of water and an alcoholic drink.

**The hosts accept the gift**, give thanks and give identical gifts of their own to welcome and seat the Guests.

**The host will continue with the question**, who are you? Where do you come from? And what brought you here?

**INTRODUCTIONS AND THE SECOND SETS OF ENVELOPES**. Guest's spokesperson, always through the Primary Host, answers: before we answer your question, may you permit us to greet you and your family? The greetings are done when given the permission.

- First envelope, 1A, greet the Primary Host,
- Second envelope, 2A, greet the Host's spokesperson.
- Third envelope, 3A, the eldest of the Hosts.
- Fourth envelope, 4A, elder men of the house or village.

- Fifth envelope, 5A, elder women.
- Sixth envelope, 6A, area/town chief,
- Seventh envelope, 7A, Mammy Queen,
- Eighth envelope, 8A, area Imam (or those who prayed to begin the meeting).
- Ninth envelope, 9A, area Pastor
- Tenth envelope, 10A, for both young men and women. And
- Eleventh envelope, 11A, children of the house.

After giving thank you, the Hosting family will repeat the previous questions and wait for the Guests to respond.

## SESSION THREE: INTRODUCTIONS OF BOTH SIDES OF THE FAMILY MEMBERS FOLLOWED BY BRINGING IN THE GROOM.

Guest's spokesperson: We will now introduce ourselves and then we will present the purpose of our visit. **GUESTS ARE INTRODUCED FOLLOWED IMMEDIATELY BY THE HOSTS INTRODUCING THEMSELVES.**

Guest's spokesperson continues and gives the envelopes to the Primary Host for the family and then concludes: **WE HAVE SEEN A WOMAN/ FLOWER IN THIS HOUSE THAT WE WANT.**

**Hosts**: who wants the woman? You?

**Guests:** Yes, but it is this man and this woman who want this woman for their son.

**Hosts to the new god parents**: Is that true? where is your son? The son is brought in with dances and seated.

## SESSION FOUR: QUESTIONS, ANSWERS, MEETING THE BIOLOGICAL PARENTS AND GOD PARENTS.

**Guests.** This is my son.

**Hosts**: Your name? Did you send this people? Who are your biological parents? They are presented. And the Hosts go on, turning to the young man. Are you married? Children? Do you work? Etc. The Hosts turning to the Primary Host will ask: do you know which woman in our house you said you want? Will you recognize her? This question might be a trap. The normal answer is, I will recognize her when I see her, but I do not know her. Saying that one knows her before may trigger fines and additional expenditure for having corrupted their daughter.

## THE GOD PARENTS AND BIOLOGICAL PARENTS ARE PRESENTED. THE HOSTS WECOME THEM WITH SOME ENVELOPES.

**THE BRIDE IS BROUGHT IN**. After series of other women have been brought in and gently rejected, the Bride is brought in. The Guests may select to ask a few questions of the bride or simply let it go.

## SESSION FIVE: THE BIOLOGICAL PARENTS AND GOD MOTHER OF THE BRIDE ARE INTRODUCED.

**Guests spokesperson**; after dancing and spraying the woman with money, the spokesperson will then ask: to whom will I marry this woman-gods parents? And who are the biological parents?

**Hosts**: Before introducing the biological parents, I will like to inform you of the following **qualities of our daughter**: she does not know how to cook, make bed, sweep the house and she does not like to have sex. The Guest's spokesperson will answer to each statement, **I WANT HER**. These are the god father and god mother. these are the biological parents.

After that, the people are introduced. this is the guard mother who brought the woman up. **Guests give them the special recognitions they deserve. The Hosts may go further to ask questions such as: What do you want this woman for. (IN THE OLDEN DAYS, IT WAS CUSTIRMARY FOR THE HOSTS TO ASK THE GROOM HIMSELF LOOKING DIECTLY AT HIM: IS THIS THE WOMAN YOU WANT? WHAT DO YOU WANT HER FOR? THE ANSWER WOULD BE SEX. UNTIL THE ARRIVAL OF MODERN DAYS, SEX WAS VERY PIVATAL IN TRADITIONAL AND CULTURAL MARRIAGES. It used to be the case that in the Mende tradition, a woman or man may sue the other for refusing her or him sex (for wasting her time-"maa bgae nyanei").**

It may be forbidden to ask that question today without offending someone or some laws. That is ok too.

## SESSION SIX: FINAL STEPS TO MARRY THE WOMAN. THIRD AND FINAL SETS OF ENVELOPES.

**Guests**: through you Sir, I want this woman for love. Gives the envelope marked **1B to the Primary Hosts.** He, in turn, gives it to the god father of the bride. God father gives it to the god mother. Looking at the bride, the god mother asks the bride: this people are asking you in love, will you accept their love proposal? I am going the envelope to you. If you accept them, then you will accept the envelope **AND ANSWER LOUDLY YES** and then give it back to me. If you do not accept their love proposal, then you will not accept the envelope **OR YOU MAY ANSWER NO.** Then I will give their envelope back to them. When the woman accepts the envelope, **there should be jubilations**. Then the second envelope marked **2B** is given to engage the woman. Then the last sets of greetings envelopes are distributed:

Third envelope, 3B, for the biological mother.

Fourth envelope, 4B, biological father.

Fifth envelope, 5B, god mother,

Sixth envelope, 6B, god father,

Seventh envelope, 7B, Guardian mother,

Eighth envelope, 8B, grandmother,

Ninth envelope, 9B. grandfather,

Tenth envelope, 10B, sisters,

Eleventh envelope, 11B, brothers,

Twelfth envelope, 12B, maternal uncles,

Thirteenth envelope, 13B, paternal uncles,

Fourteenth envelope, 14B, aunts,

Fifteenth envelope, 15B, friends and

Sixteenth envelope, 16B, all other relatives not present today.

**Guest**: wait for a final response. The guests may select to ask the woman few clarification questions. Be careful not to anger the woman or her family.

**Hosts**: The hosts should greet the biological parents and god parents of the groom with some envelopes.

**Guests:** The Calabash, brought by a teenage girl, is first given by the groom's god father to the bride's god mother. She takes it. Ask the bride whether the family is to accept the Calabash on her behalf. If she answers yes, the god mother will then give the Calabash to the bride. She will take it and then give it back to the god mother to show her final approve. The Calabash is then taken to a secret location and the content checked. If accepted, the family members will return with jubilation and dancing.

**LAST SESSION**: The final envelope marked 17B, is given to ask for the woman to move into the husband's house.

This is the end.

THAT'S ALL AND THAT'S THE WAY I SEE IT.

THANK YOU.


Name: Lansana Nyalley. Sign: _____

Date: _____

Printed in the United States
By Bookmasters